World War I
Cumulative Index

World War I
Cumulative Index

Cumulates Indexes For:

World War I: Almanac

World War I: Biographies

World War I: Primary Sources

Allison McNeill,

Index Coordinator

GALE GROUP

™

THOMSON LEARNING

Detroit • New York • San Diego • San Francisco
Boston • New Haven, Conn. • Waterville, Maine
London • Munich

Allison McNeill, *Index Coordinator*

Cover photographs: Woodrow Wilson, United States Army Signal Corps (AP/Wide World Photos. Reproduced by permission.); Propaganda poster, Celebrating the Armistice (Corbis Corporation. Reproduced by permission.)

Library of Congress Control Number: 2001096320

ISBN 0-7876-5479-5

Printed in the United States of America

10 9 8 7 6 5 4 3 2 1

Cumulative Index

A = *World War I: Almanac*
B = *World War I: Biographies*
PS = *World War I: Primary Sources*

A

Aaronsohn, Sarah
 B: 1–5, 1 (ill.)
Abd el-Krim
 B: 129
Aces (figher pilots)
 A: 148–151
 Bishop, William Avery **B:** 13–18
 Richthofen, Manfred von; (the Red Baron) **B:** 13–14, 17, 132–37
 Rickenbacker, Eddie **B:** 138–43
AEF. *See* American Expeditionary Forces
Africa, battles in
 A: 106 (ill.), 107–109, 122
African American soldiers
 B: 120
African Americans, treatment and role of, during WWI
 A: 177, 180 (ill.), 182–183
Agreements. *See* Alliances; Armistice agreements; Treaties
Airplanes
 A: 148 (ill.), 207 (ill.)
 PS: 23, 24 (ill.), 26 (ill.)
 bombs dropped by **A:** 107, 147, 148, 167
 number of planes used in WWI **A:** 75–77
 poison gas dropped by **A:** 142
 role of, in WWI **A:** 59, 137, 147–151
 used during World War II **A:** 153
 used to combat submarines **A:** 135
Aisne, First Battle of the
 A: 41
 PS: 119
Aisne, Second Battle of the
 A: 58, 59–61
Albania
 A: 13
Albert I
 A: 29
 PS: 76
Aleppo
 B: 7
Alexander II
 B: 36
Alexander III
 B: 36

Boldface type indicates abbreviation of individual titles

Bold numerals indicate main entries

Illustrations are marked by (ill.)

Alexandra (Russian czarina)
A: 95, 98–99, 100 (ill.)
B: **34–41**, 34 (ill.), 37 (ill.)
Alexis (son of Nicholas II)
A: 98, 100 (ill.)
Algeciras Conference of 1906
A: 13
All Quiet on the Western Front
PS: 113, 114, **131–133**,
134–143, **140** (ill.), **144**, 145
Allenby, Edmund
A: 118
B: 5, 87
Alliances
Allies A: 1
Austro-Hungarian A: 4–5
British A: 7
Central Powers A: 1, 11
Dual Alliance A: 1, 5, 10, 14;
PS: 50, 51, 53–54, **55–57**,
58, 59
Entente Cordiale A: 7
Franco-Russian Alliance
Military Convention
PS: 51, 54, 55, **57–58**, 59
French A: 3, 5–6, 7
German A: 3–5
League of the Three Emperors
A: 3, 5
Reinsurance Treaty of 1887 A: 3
role of, in starting WWI
PS: 49–50, 53–54, 58
Russian A: 3, 5–6, 7
Triple Alliance PS: 50, 59
Triple Entente A: 1, 7, 10, 11,
14
Allies
A: 1, 57, 105
B: 169, 173–76
PS: 17, 81, 82
casualty rate and soldiers killed
in combat A: 199, 200;
PS: 38, 47
final offensives of the A: 73–81
first major attacks by the
A: 36 (ill.)
Greece and the A: 102
Italy and the A: 118
members of PS: 79
naval strategy of the A: 123,
127–130, 135, 151–153.
(*See also* War plans; Western
Front: strategy used on the)

peace terms dictated by the
A: 189–195
U.S. support and sympathy for
PS: 80, 87, 91
Alsace-Lorraine region
B: 49
PS: 71, 107
French attacks in A: 31, 36
history of dispute over A: 3
peace terms regarding A: 191
strategic importance of A: 25,
26, 29, 30
Ambulances on the Italian front
PS: 147 (ill.)
America. *See* United States
American Expeditionary Forces
(AEF)
B: 118, 123, 169, 173, 175
American Protective League
A: 177
American Red Cross
B: 23
PS: 88, 146, 147 (ill.), 171, 183
American troops in Europe
during WWI
B: 103, 122
See also American Expeditionary
Forces
Amiens
A: 69, 75, 147
Anastasia
B: 40
Anatolia
A: 112
B: 3
PS: 32
Anderson, Anna
B: 40
Anthem for Doomed Youth
PS: **124–125**
Anti-Jewish attitudes in Europe
B: 1–2, 65, 69
See also Jewish people:
persecution of, in Europe
Anti-Semitism
B: 2, 65, 69
PS: 198
Antiwar sentiments in Europe
A: 12–13, 14, 99, 101
Anzacs
A: 114–115
Arab independence, British
promises of
B: 86–88

Ardennes
  A: 37
Armenians, genocide of
  A: 111, 112, 198
  B: 3
  PS: 32–33, 37
Armies, size of European
  A: 9–12
Armistice agreements
  A: 82, 83, 101, 103, 193–194
Armistice celebrations (ill.)
  A: 191, 192, 195
Armistice ending WWI
  B: 169, 174
  PS: 37, 39, 44 (ill.)
  See also World War I: end of
Arras, Battle of
  A: 62
  B: 113, 158
Artillery. See Weapons: artillery
Artois, First Battle of
  A: 41
Artois, Third Battle of
  A: 47
Asquith, Herbert
  A: 57
Atatürk, Mustafa Kemal
  A: 114, 208
  B: 6–12, 6 (ill.), 10 (ill.)
Atbara, battle of
  B: 56
Attrition, war of
  A: 44
Australia, role of, in WWI
  A: 75, 107, 114–115, 199
Australian and New Zealand Army
    Corps (Anzacs)
  A: 114–115
Austria, recruiting poster from
  PS: 177 (ill.)
Austria-Hungary
  A: 4.
  B: 42, 44
  PS: 55, 103
  alliances of A: 4–5; PS: 50,
    53–54
  annexation of Bosnia and
    Herzegovina A: 13
  borders of, 1914 (ill.) A: 18
  casualty rate and soldiers killed
    in combat A: 199, 200;
    PS: 38–39
  collapse of A: 103–104

conflict with Serbia A: 13, 16,
    19–23, 91–92
  ethnic divisions within A: 5, 82,
    101, 103
  goals of, in WWI A: 203
  industry and manufacturing in
    A: 6
  military and naval strength of
    A: 6, 10, 11
  population A: 6
  Serbia's conflict with PS: 58–59,
    61, 63, 64, 69
  war plans A: 26, 92
Austro-Hungarian Empire. See
    Austria-Hungary
Aviation. See Aces (fighter pilots);
    Airplanes; Reconnaissance
    (information-gathering)
    missions

B

Babeuf, François-Noël
  B: 63
Baden, Prince of (Maximilian)
  A: 83
Baghdad
  A: 116
Baker, Newton
  B: 29
Balfour Declaration
  B: 5
Balkan states and provinces
    (the Balkans)
  A: 13, 14, 15, 19, 21
  PS: 54, 55, 63
Balkan Wars
  A: 194
Barbed wire. See Weapons:
    barbed wire
Basra
  A: 115
Battle conditions
  B: 116 (ill.)
  PS: 136–142 (fiction), 152–154
    (fiction) (see also Trench
    warfare)
  British soldiers' perspective on
    PS: 20–21, 28–31
  food shortage PS: 31
  German soldiers' perspective on
    PS: 21–22, 27–28, 31–34

nurses' perspective on
  PS: 39–42
shell shock caused by **PS:** 34
Battles
  Aisne, First Battle of the **A:** 41;
    PS: 119
  Aisne, Second Battle of the
    A: 58, 59–61
  Arras **A:** 62
  Artois, First Battle of **A:** 41
  Artois, Third Battle of **A:** 47
  Brusilov Offensive
    A: 96–97 (ill.)
  Cambrai **A:** 65, 146–147
  Caporetto **A:** 120
  Champagne, First Battle of
    A: 44; **PS:** 119
  Champagne, Second Battle of
    A: 47
  Coronel **A:** 125
  Dogger Bank **A:** 130
  Falklands, the **A:** 125
  final Allied offensive **A:** 73–81
  final German offensive (spring
    offensive) **A:** 67, 68–73,
    74 (ill.)
  first major attacks of WWI
    (ill.) **A:** 36
  Gallipoli **A:** 113–115, 122
  Heligoland Bight **A:** 130
  Isonzo, the **A:** 120
  Jutland **A:** 130–132 (ill.)
  location of (war zones)
    A: 106 (ill.), 111 (ill.)
  Loos **A:** 47–48, 139
  Lys **A:** 69, 70
  Marne, the **A:** 39–40 (ill.)
  Masuria, Winter Battle of **A:** 91
  Megiddo **A:** 118
  Messines **PS:** 28–30
  Meuse-Argonne, the
    A: 77–80 (ill.)
  Mons **A:** 37, 38–39
  Mörhange-Sarrebourg **A:** 137
  naval **A:** 113, 123–135 (ill.)
  Passchendaele **A:** 63–65
  race to the sea **A:** 40–41
  Serre **PS:** 123
  Somme, the **A:** 49, 52–54, 79;
    PS: 20–21, 21–27, 119
  spring offensive **A:** 67, 68–73
  Tannenberg **A:** 88–90 (ill.), 94
  Verdun **A:** 49–51

war zones during WWI
  A: 106 (ill.), 111 (ill.)
weather conditions affecting
  A: 63, 92–93, 108, 111,
  113, 116
Ypres (First) **A:** 41
Ypres (Second) **A:** 45, 46
Ypres (Third) **A:** 63–65;
  PS: 27–28
See also Africa; Middle East;
  Pacific; Turkey (battles in)
Battleships. *See* Weapons:
  battleships; Weapons:
  dreadnoughts
BEF. *See* British Expeditionary
  Force
Belgian army, size of
  PS: 78
Belgium
  PS: 51, 68, 71–73, 74 (ill.), 76
  allies of **A:** 9–10
  casualties **A:** 42, 199
  invasion of **A:** 24, 29, 32–35
  war resistance movement in
    B: 22, 24–25
Belgium's Response to the Request
  for Passage
  PS: 51, 75–76
Belleau Wood
  A: 181
  PS: 98
Below Saleske, Herr von
  PS: 73
Berger, Victor
  B: 82
Bethmann Hollweg,
  Theobald von
  A: 83
  B: 101
Billik, Paul
  B: 17
Bishop, William "Billy" Avery
  B: 13–18, 13 (ill.)
Bismarck Archipelago
  A: 107
Bismarck, Otto von
  A: 2, 3, 4 (ill.)
  B: 165, 167
Black Hand, the
  A: 16, 17, 20, 21
  B: 45
Black soldiers. *See* African
  Americans, treatment and
  role of, during WWI

Blockade, naval
  A: 67, 123, 129, 151,
    162–163, 173
Blockade of Germany
  PS: 80, 87, 92, 93, 170
Bloody Sunday
  PS: 191
Blunden, Edmund
  B: 117
  PS: 117
Boer War (1899–1902)
  A: 39
  B: 56, 147
Bolsheviks
  A: 100, 101, 205
  B: 82, 93–94
  PS: 213, 214
Bombing, ruins caused by
  A: 82 (ill.), 160 (ill.)
Bombs. *See* Airplanes: bombs
    dropped by; Weapons:
    bombs, mines, and explosives
Bonds. *See* War bonds
Bosnia and Herzegovina
  A: 13, 16, 20, 194
  B: 42, 46
  PS: 63
Bowles, J.
  PS: 28–30
Boy Scouts of America
  PS: 171, 212–213
Brahms, Johannes
  B: 78
Brest-Litovsk, Treaty of
  A: 94
  PS: 214
Britain. *See* Great Britain
British Commonwealth
    of Nations
  B: 16
British Expeditionary Force (BEF)
  A: 27, 30, 37–39, 43, 48
  B: 56–57
  PS: 17
Brooke, Rupert
  B: 112–13
  PS: 113, 116 (ill.), 118, 123
  attitude of, toward WWI
    PS: 118
  background and war experience
    of PS: 116, 128, 130
  poems by PS: 118–120
  popularity of poems by
    PS: 122

Bruckner, Anton
  B: 78
Brusilov, Aleksey
  A: 96
Brusilov Offensive
  A: 96–97 (ill.)
Bulgaria
  A: 13
  PS: 63
  armistice signed by A: 82,
    102–103
  casualties A: 199
  peace treaty terms regarding
    A: 194–195
  strategic role of, in WWI A: 92
Bull Moose Party (U.S.)
  B: 172
Burleson, Albert
  A: 176
Byng, Julian
  A: 62

C

Cabrinovic, Nedeljko
  A: 20
Cadorna, Luigi
  A: 120
Cambrai, Battle of
  A: 65, 146–147
Cameroons
  A: 107, 108, 195
Canada, role of, in WWI
  A: 62, 75, 199
  B: 16
Capitalism
  PS: 191
Capitalists
  B: 71
Caporetto, Battle of
  A: 120
  PS: 161
Caprivi, Leo von
  B: 165
Carl Ludvig
  B: 43
Carol I
  A: 97
Carolines, the
  A: 107
Carpathian Mountains
  A: 110 (ill.)
Cartoons. *See* Political cartoons

Casualties
　　A: 33 (ill.), 60 (ill.), 200 (ill.)
　　PS: 34, 38–39
　　casualty rates A: 200
　　deaths in combat A: 199
　　See also Deaths caused by WWI
Caucasus Mountains
　　A: 110
Cavalry in WWI
　　A: 28
　　B: 14, 58, 133
Cavell, Edith
　　B: **19–26**, 19 (ill.), 21 (ill.)
　　funeral of B: 24 (ill.)
Cemal Paśa, Ahmed
　　A: 117
Cemeteries for WWI soldiers
　　A: 202 (ill.), 209 (ill.)
Censorship during WWI
　　A: 159, 160
　　B: 27, 29, 122
　　PS: 12, 169
Central Powers
　　A: 1, 11, 105, 194
　　B: 169, 173
　　PS: 17, 77, 81, 82, 102
　　army size of PS: 14
　　attack on Serbia by A: 92–93
　　casualty rate and soldiers
　　　　killed in combat A: 199, 200;
　　　　PS: 38
　　collapse of A: 81–83
　　Italian retreat forced by PS: 161
　　members of PS: 79
　　naval strategy of A: 123,
　　　　133–135. (*See also* War plans;
　　　　Western Front: strategy
　　　　used on the)
　　number of deaths among PS: 47
　　surrender of A: 103
　　U.S. trade with PS: 80
Champagne, First Battle of
　　A: 44
　　PS: 119
Champagne, Second Battle of
　　A: 47
Chapman, Guy
　　PS: 13
Charleroi
　　B: 22
Charles I
　　A: 101
Cheka (Russian secret police)
　　B: 93

Chemical warfare
　　A: 46
　　See also Poison gas
Chemin des Dames
　　A: 71
Child labor laws (U.S.)
　　PS: 102
Christmas Truce
　　A: 42
Churchill, Winston
　　A: 113
Civilian attitudes toward WWI
　　early in the war A: 12–13, 14,
　　　　24, 28–29
　　in Austria-Hungary A: 101
　　in Germany A: 161, 169
　　in Russia A: 93, 99
　　in the United States
　　　　A: 171–172, 174, 176, 177
Civilian war effort
　　A: 155–169
Civilians, effects of WWI on
　　PS: 47, 163–166
　　bombings A: 82 (ill.), 147
　　deaths A: 198, 200
　　food shortage A: 129, 161–164
　　refugees A: 157 (ill.),
　　　　163 (ill.), 200
　　See also Civilian war effort
Clemenceau, Georges
　　A: 27, 158, 190 (ill.), 191
　　B: 174, 174 (ill.)
Cold War, the
　　A: 206
Colonies, WWI fighting in
　　European
　　A: 106–109
Committee on Public
　　Information (CPI)
　　A: 177
　　B: 27, 29–33
　　PS: 99
Commonwealth of Nations
　　B: 16
Communism
　　A: 206.
　　B: 70, 90–91, 95, 145
　　See also Russia: communist
　　　　control in
Communist Party
　　B: 64, 82
Conrad von Hötzendorf, Franz
　　A: 20, 90

Conscientious objectors
  B: 180
Conscription (military draft)
  A: 10, 76, 155–156, 180, 181
  B: 31, 173
  PS: 8, 14, 99, 163
Conservatives
  B: 64
Constantine
  A: 102
Constantinople
  A: 112
Convoy, naval
  A: 135, 153, 175 (ill.)
Coolidge, Calvin
  B: 177
Coronel, Battle of
  A: 125
Cossacks
  A: 99
  PS: 203
Costs. *See* WWI: costs of, financial
Counter-Attack
  PS: 125–126
Cox, James M.
  B: 177
CPI. *See* Committee on Public
  Information
Creel, George
  A: 177
  B: 27–33, 27 (ill.)
Crimean War (1854–56)
  PS: 2
Czechoslovakia
  A: 194, 197, 204

D

Dadourian, Gadarinée
  PS: 32–33
Damascus
  A: 118
Dardanelles, the
  A: 110, 113, 127
Davignon, M.
  PS: 73
de Croÿ, Marie
  B: 22, 24–25
de Croÿ, Reginald
  B: 22, 24
de Gaulle, Charles
  B: 130
Dead, The
  PS: 119–120

Deaths caused by WWI
  A: 199
  PS: 37, 47
  See also Casualties caused
  by WWI
Debs, Eugene V.
  PS: 102
Declaration of Neutrality (Wilson)
  PS: 81, 86–87
Defense of the Realm Act (DORA)
  A: 161
  PS: 170
Democratic socialism
  B: 65
Depression, worldwide economic
  A: 185, 202
d'Esperey, Franchet
  A: 102
Dimitrijevic, Dragutin
  A: 21
Diplomatic messages and
  government declarations
  Belgium's Response to the
  Request for Passage
  PS: 51, 75–76
  Dual Alliance between the
  German Empire and the
  Austro-Hungarian Empire
  PS: 55–57
  Franco-Russian Alliance
  Military Convention PS: 51,
  54, 55, 57–58, 59
  German Request for Free
  Passage through Belgium
  PS: 51, 74–75
  Telegrams from American
  consulates in Russia PS: 167,
  204–211
  Willy-Nicky Telegrams PS: 51,
  61, 62, 64–68
  Woodrow Wilson's Declaration
  of Neutrality PS: 81, 86–87
  Woodrow Wilson's Fourteen
  Points PS: 82, 101–104,
  104–108
  Woodrow Wilson's War
  Message PS: 81, 94–97
Diplomats, role of
  PS: 49, 51
Disease, worldwide.
  See Spanish Flu
Dogger Bank (battle)
  A: 130

DORA. *See* Defense of the Realm
Act
Dos Passos, John
PS: 88, 161
Dostoyevsky, Fyodor
B: 70
Douaumont, Fort
A: 50, 51
B: 130
Draft, military. *See* Conscription
Dreadnoughts
A: 124 (ill.), 125, 131, 132, 151
Dreyfus, Alfred
B: 65
Dreyfus affair
B: 65
Dual Alliance, the
A: 1, 5, 10, 14
PS: 51, 55
members of **PS:** 50, 53
purpose of **PS:** 53–54, 58, 59
text of treaty signed by
PS: 55–57, 59
Dugouts. *See* Trench warfare
Dulce Et Decorum Est
PS: 126–128

E

East Prussia
A: 85, 86, 87, 88, 94
Eastern Front
B: 100–01
PS: 167
battles on the **A:** 85–94, 96–97,
101–103 (ill.)
location/extent of **A:** 85–86,
96 (ill.), 101–102
strategy on the **A:** 44, 85–86,
86–87
Ebert, Friedrich
A: 193
PS: 198
Economic changes in Europe
during WWI
PS: 163–166, 167
Economy
European, during WWI
A: 156–159
European and U.S., after WWI
A: 185, 202, 208
European and U.S., prior to
WWI **A:** 8–9

Eliot, T. S.
PS: 128
Elizabeth
(Austrian archduchess)
B: 43
Emden (battleship)
A: 125–127 (ill.)
Engels, Friedrich
B: 70
England. *See* Great Britain
Enlistment
PS: 9–10
in France **PS:** 8 (ill.)
in Germany **PS:** 134–136
(fiction)
posters used to encourage
PS: 6 (ill.), 7, 12, **172 (ill.),**
177 (ill.)
Entente Cordiale
A: 7
Entente powers.
See Triple Entente
Enver Paśa
A: 110, 111
Espionage Act, the
A: 176
Europe
antiwar sentiments in
A: 12–13, 14, 99, 101
economic changes in, during
WWI **PS:** 163–166, 167
economies after WWI
A: 202, 208
economies during WWI
A: 156–159;
economies before WWI
A: 8–9
military power in, 1914
A: 9–12
nationalism in **A:** 14
neutral countries in, during
WWI **A:** 42, 124, 129
political balance in, before
WWI **PS:** 49–50, 53–54
political boundaries of, after
Treaty of Versailles (ill.)
A: 203
political boundaries of,
in 1914 (ill.) **A:** 2
possessions of, prior to WWI
(ill.) **A:** 10
Expatriates
B: 146

A = World War I: Almanac   B = World War I: Biographies

F

Factories, production of war
   materials in
   A: 156–157, 158 (ill.), 165 (ill.),
   166 (ill.)
Factories used for war effort
   PS: 164 (ill.), 184 (ill.)
Faisal (Arab troop leader)
   B: 87
Falkenhayn, Erich von
   A: 44, 48, 51, 93, 97, 118
   B: 97
Falklands, Battle of the
   A: 125
Farewell to Arms, A
   PS: 113, 133, 145, 146–148,
   149–160, 161
Faulkner, William
   PS: 88, 161
FBI (Federal Bureau of
   Investigation)
   B: 82
Federal Reserve System
   B: 172
   PS: 103
Federal Trade Commission
   B: 172
   PS: 103
Feinberg, Absalom
   B: 3
Ferdinand, Franz. *See* Franz
   Ferdinand.
Ferdinand I
   A: 92
Fez, banning of the
   B: 9–10
*First World War: An Eyewitness
   History*
   PS: 10
Fitzgerald, F. Scott
   PS: 135
Flamethrower
   A: 49, 50, 121 (ill.), 144
Flanders
   A: 42
Flu, Spanish
   A: 169
Flying Circus, the
   B: 14, 134 (ill.), 135
Foch, Ferdinand
   A: 69 (ill.), 73, 77, 79, 181,
   207–208
   B: **48–53**, 48 (ill.), 51 (ill.), 127
   PS: 176 (ill.)

Fokker, Anthony
   A: 149
Fokker DVII (fighter plane)
   PS: 24 (ill.)
Fonck, Paul-René
   A: 149
Food production during WWI
   PS: 187
Food shortage during WWI
   A: 161–164, 178
   B: 160 (ill.)
   among civilians PS: 37, 165
   among troops in battle PS: 31
   in Germany PS: 93, 142
   (fiction)
   in Great Britain PS: 202 (ill.)
   in Russia PS: 167, 202–203,
   205, 207
Fort Douaumont
   A: 50, 51
Fort Vaux
   A: 50, 51
Fourteen Points address (Wilson)
   A: 182–183, 187, 188, 190,
   192, 196
   B: 31, 169, 173
   PS: 82, 101–104, **104–108**
France
   alliances of A: 3, 5–6, 7, 24;
   PS: 50, 54 (ill.), 58, 59
   army revolt of French soldiers
   A: 61–62, 157, 161
   casualty rate and soldiers
   killed in combat A: 52 (ill.),
   199, 200
   colonies of A: 107, 204
   conscription (military draft) in
   PS: 8
   economy of, during WWI
   PS: 201–202
   goals of, in WWI A: 203
   government of, before WWI
   A: 5–6
   industry and manufacturing in
   A: 7, 156–158
   military and economic strength
   of, before WWI PS: 54
   military and naval strength of
   A: 7, 9, 11
   optimism in, at beginning of
   WWI PS: 6–7
   population of A: 7

propaganda posters in **PS:** 174
(ill.), 176 (ill.), 179 (ill.),
186 (ill.)
recruiting posters in
PS: 7, 174 (ill.)
soldiers (ill.) **A:** 35, 40, 52, 152
strikes in **PS:** 215
war plans **A:** 26–27, 44, 45
See also French army
Franco, Francisco
B: 129
Franco-Prussian War (1870–71)
A: 3, 5, 159
B: 49–50
PS: 2, 53
Franco-Russian Alliance Military
Convention
PS: 51, 54, 55, **57–58**, 59
Frantz, Joseph
A: 148, 151
Franz Ferdinand
A: 1, 15, 16–18, 19, 91
B: 42–47, 42 (ill.), 44 (ill.)
PS: 1, 50 (ill.), 58, 63
Franz Josef I
A: 4, 5 (ill.), 19, 22, 101
PS: 63
Frederick the Great.
See Friedrich II
French, John
B: 56–57
French, Sir John
A: 37
French army
casualty rate of **PS:** 39
mutiny of **PS:** 170, 214
size of **PS:** 8
French Foreign Legion
B: 144, 146
PS: 88, 119, 130
French Socialist Party
B: 65
Freud, Sigmund
B: 78
Fribourg, André
PS: 10
Friedrich I
B: 167
Friedrich II (Frederick the Great)
B: 167
Friedrich III
B: 164, 167
Frost, Robert
B: 113, 158–59

Fuel for heat, shortage of,
during WWI
A: 161–162
Fyodorovna, Alexandra. *See*
Alexandra (Russian czarina)

G

Galicia
A: 85, 90, 91, 100
Gallipoli
A: 113–115, 122
B: 7
PS: 2, 116
Garros, Roland
A: 148, 149–151
Gas attacks. *See* Poison gas
Gas masks
A: 142 (ill.), 143
PS: 40 (ill.)
Genocide of Armenians
A: 111, 112, 198
B: 3
PS: 32–33, 37
George. *See* Lloyd George, David
George V
B: 166
German Americans, treatment
of, during WWI
A: 177
German army
casualty rate of. *See* Central
Powers: casualty rate of
crossing Belgium **PS:** 74 (ill.)
morale of **PS:** 41–43
mutinies of **PS:** 215
retreat of **PS:** 142–143 (fiction)
size of **PS:** 8
soldiers from **PS:** 77 (ill.),
137 (ill.)
German Communist Party
PS: 197
German East Africa
A: 107, 108–109
German Empire
A: 3
PS: 53, 55
German New Guinea
A: 107
German Request for Free Passage
through Belgium
PS: 51, **74–75**

German Southwest Africa
  A: 107, 108
German Workers' Party
  A: 206
Germany
  alliances of A: 3–5; PS: 50,
    53–54
  armistice signed by A: 83,
    193–194; B: 103
  blockade of PS: 80, 87, 92,
    93, 170
  borders of, 1914 (ill.) A: 18
  casualties A: 199
  colonies of A: 106–109, 194,
    195
  conscription (military draft)
    in PS: 8
  declaration of war by
    PS: 68, 72 (ill.)
  economy of, during WWI A: 8,
    192, 197, 202 ; PS: 201
  first major attacks by A: 36 (ill.)
  food shortage in PS: 93, 142
    (fiction)
  goals of, in WWI A: 202–203
  industry and manufacturing in
    A: 3, 12, 156–159
  militarism and expansionist
    policy in B: 167
  military strength of A: 3, 10, 11,
    12; PS: 53–54
  modernization and
    industrialization in
    B: 163, 165
  naval strength and strategy
    A: 11, 123–129, 133–135
  population of A: 3
  propaganda posters in
    PS: 180 (ill.)
  punishment of, after WWI
    A: 204; PS: 108, 110
  railway system in PS: 14, 72
  recruiting posters in PS: 7
  revolution in B: 150–52, 154–55
  soldiers (ill.) A: 17, 38, 43,
    89, 195
  spring offensive launched by
    A: 67, 68–73, 74 (ill.); B: 60,
    102–03
  strikes in PS: 215
  surrender of PS: 98, 109 (ill.)
  telegram sent to Mexico by
    PS: 93
  Treaty of Versailles A: 193–194

  war plans A: 24–26 (Schlieffen
    plan), 44, 48, 68–69; PS: 51,
    71–73
  See also German army
Geronimo
  B: 119
Gestapo
  B: 74
Ghost Dance Rebellion
  B: 119
Goethe, Johann Wolfgang von
  B: 70
Good-Bye to All That
  PS: 21, 30–31
Gorky, Maksim
  B: 70
Gorlice
  A: 93
Grady, Tom
  PS: 45
Graves, Robert
  B: 89, 112–13, 115
  PS: 19, 21, 30–31, 117
Great Britain
  alliances of A: 7; PS: 50, 59
  blockade of Germany by PS: 80,
    87, 92, 93, 170
  casualty rate of A: 199 (see also
    Allies: casualty rate of)
  colonies of A: 6, 107, 204
  conscription (military draft) in
    PS: 8, 14
  economy of, during WWI A: 6;
    PS: 201–202
  expeditionary force from A: 27,
    30, 37–39, 43, 48
  food shortage in PS: 202 (ill.)
  goals of, in WWI A: 203
  industry and manufacturing in
    A: 9, 156
  military and naval strength of
    A: 9, 10, 11
  morale of soldiers from
    PS: 20–21, 28–30
  navy A: 7, 11, 44, 113,
    123–124, 125
  pilots from PS: 26 (ill.)
  population of A: 9
  propaganda posters in
    PS: 182 (ill.), 184 (ill.)
  recruiting posters in
    PS: 7, 172 (ill.)
  soldiers (ill.) A: 191
  strikes in PS: 215

war plans of **A:** 27, 43–44
women's voting rights in
PS: 187
Great Depression, the
A: 185, 202
B: 33
Great War, The. *See* World War I
Greece
A: 13, 102
PS: 63
Gregory, Thomas W.
A: 176
Guns. *See* Weapons: artillery;
Weapons: machine guns
Guynemer, Georges-Marie
A: 149

H

Habsburgs
B: 43
Haig, Douglas
A: 44 (ill.), 47, 49, 52–54,
63, 70, 80
B: 54–61, 54 (ill.), 57(ill.)
Haldane, Richard
B: 56
Hardaumont
B: 130
Harding, Constanza
B: 72
Harding, Warren G.
B: 177
Hauptmann, Gerhart
B: 70
Hawker, Lanoe
B: 135
Hay, W.
PS: 20–21
Heligoland Bight, Battle of
A: 130
Hemingway, Ernest
PS: 2, 113, 114, **145–148,**
146 (ill.)
novels by **PS:** 161
postwar attitude reflected in
war novels by **PS:** 128,
133, 148
success of **PS:** 161
WWI service of **PS:** 88, 145–146
Hertling, Georg von
A: 73

Herzegovina.
See Bosnia-Herzegovina
Herzl, Theodor
B: 4
Hindenburg, Paul von
A: 51, 73, 87 (ill.), 88, 89,
90, 147
B: 97, 100–104, 100 (ill.)
Hindenburg line
A: 59, 74 (ill.), 81
PS: 123
Hipper, Franz von
A: 130, 131
Hitler, Adolf
A: 28, 76, 112, 193, 197,
206–207, 208
PS: 110
as leader of Nazi Party
B: 69, 83, 130
condemned by George Creel
B: 33
Ludendorff's association with
B: 104
Wilhelm II's association with
B: 167–68
Hohenzollern
B: 164, 167
Home front, war effort on the
A: 155–169
PS: 163–166, 178 (ill.)
Hoover, Herbert
A: 178
Hoover, J. Edgar
B: 82
Horses, mobilization and the
use of
A: 28, 156
Hôtel des Invalides
B: 50
Hötzendorf. *See* Conrad von
Hötzendorf, Franz
Howitzer (ill.)
A: 32
Hughes, Charles Evans
B: 173
Humanitarian organizations,
assistance of, during WWI
B: 23
Humanitarians
Cavell, Edith **B:** 19–26
Kollwitz, Käthe **B:** 68–76
York, Alvin C. **B:** 178–83
Husayn ibn 'Alî
B: 87

I

I Have a Rendezvous with Death
  PS: 120
Ibsen, Henrik
  B: 70
Imperial War Conference (1917)
  B: 16
Imperialism
  PS: 80, 192
Industrial Revolution
  B: 63
Industrialization
  A: 6, 97, 153
Industry and manufacturing
  in Austria-Hungary **A:** 6
  in France **A:** 7, 156–158
  in Germany **A:** 3, 12, 156–159
  in Great Britain **A:** 9, 156
  in Russia **A:** 12
  in United States **A:** 14
  See also Factories, production
    of war materials in
International Socialist Bureau
    Congress (1903)
  PS: 191
International Women's Day
  PS: 203
Internationalists
  A: 183
  PS: 109
Islam
  B: 9, 11
Isolationists and isolationism
  A: 183–184, 185, 196, 208
  PS: 80, 82, 83, 103, 109
Isonzo, Battles of the
  A: 120
Israel
  B: 1, 5
Italian army
  PS: 155 (ill.)
  attitude of soldiers in
    PS: 149–150 (fiction)
  harshness of **PS:** 148,
    156–159 (fiction)
  retreat of **PS:** 145, 156–159
    (fiction), 161–162
Italian front
  PS: 145, 146, 147 (ill.)
Italy
  alliances of **PS:** 50
  casualties **A:** 199
  goals of, in WWI **A:** 191

location/extent of Italian Front
    A: 118 (ill.), 120
  political changes in, after WWI
    A: 208
  role of, in WWI **A:** 105,
    118–121, 122
  soldiers **A:** 119 (ill.)

J

Jagerstatter, Franz
  B: 180
Japan, role of, in WWI
  A: 107
Jaurès, Jean
  B: 62–67, 62 (ill.), 66 (ill.)
Jellicoe, Sir John
  A: 132
Jerusalem
  A: 118
Jewish people
  homeland proposed for
    B: 4–5, 87
  hostility toward **PS:** 198
  persecution of, in Europe
    B: 1–2, 4, 65, 75, 129
Joffre, Joseph
  A: 26, 35, 37, 39 (ill.), 45,
    46, 51, 58
  B: 130
Jogiches, Leo
  PS: 190, 198
Jünger, Ernst
  PS: 20, 31–34, 42–43
Junius Pamphlet
  PS: 167, 191, **192–197**
Jutland, Battle of
  A: 130–132 (ill.)

K

Kemal, Mustafa. *See* Atatürk,
    Mustafa Kemal
Kemalists
  B: 11
Kiaochow
  A: 107
Kilmer, Joyce
  B: 147
Kingsley, Charles
  B: 63

Klinger, Max
B: 70
Kluck, Alexander von
A: 38
Kollwitz, Käthe
B: 68–76, 68 (ill.)
Königsberg
A: 87
Kreibohm, Gottfried
PS: 21–22
Kreisler, Fritz
B: 32, 77–83, 77 (ill.), 80 (ill.)
Kressenstein, Franz Kress von
A: 117
Kurdish rebellion in Turkey
B: 11
Kut
A: 116, 117

L

Labor protests
A: 157–158, 163–164, 176
B: 40, 64, 82, 93
PS: 167, 191, 203, 215
Ladoux, Georges
B: 108, 110
Lafayette, Marquis de
B: 118
Landship. See Weapons: tanks
Lanrezac, Charles
A: 37
Lansing, Robert
B: 29, 32
Lausanne, Treaty of
B: 9
Lawrence, T. E. (Lawrence
of Arabia)
B: 84–89, 84 (ill.), 86 (ill.)
Le Cateau
A: 39
League of Nations
A: 183–185, 188, 195, 196
B: 16, 169, 173, 175–76
PS: 82, 103, 104, 109, 110
League of the Three Emperors
A: 3, 5
Left, the
B: 64–65
Leftists
B: 64, 69, 82
Lenin, Vladimir Ilich
A: 101, 205, 206

B: 82, 90–96, 90 (ill.),
94 (ill.), 102
PS: 214
Lettow-Vorbeck, Paul von
A: 109
Lewis, Cecil
PS: 20, 22–27, 37
Liberals
B: 64
Liberty Bonds/Loans
B: 30 (ill.), 32
PS: 166, 169, 173 (ill.), 174 (ill.),
175 (ill.), 176 (ill.), 181 (ill.)
posters promoting purchase of
A: 161 (ill.), 173 (ill.), 179
Liebknecht, Karl
PS: 197, 198
Liège
A: 29, 33
B: 99
PS: 76
Limy
A: 78 (ill.)
Lines of Fire: Women Writers
of World War I
PS: 32–33, 39–42
Lishansky, Yosef
B: 3
Literature
after WWI PS: 128
importance of, during WWI
PS: 115
Lloyd George, David
A: 14, 58, 190 (ill.), 191, 192
B: 58–59, 174 (ill.), 175
Location of WWI battles
(war zones)
A: 106 (ill.), 111 (ill.).
See also Battles
Lodge, Henry Cabot
A: 184, 185
B: 176
Loos, Battle of
A: 47–48, 139
Lorraine. See Alsace-Lorraine
region
Lost Battalion, the (U.S. troops)
A: 79–80
Ludendorff, Erich
A: 51, 67–69, 71–72, 73, 76, 83,
87 (ill.), 88, 89, 90
B: 97–104, 97 (ill.), 100 (ill.)
Lusitania
A: 133, 152, 173

B: 147, 172
  PS: 7, 92 (ill.)
Luxembourg
  A: 24, 25
  PS: 71
Luxemburg, Rosa
  PS: 166–167, **189–192,**
    190 (ill.), 197, 198
Lys, Battle of
  A: 69, 70
Lys River
  A: 41

M

Machine guns, use of,
    during WWI
  B: 58
  PS: 17–18
  See also Weapons: machine
    guns
Mackensen, August von
  A: 93, 94
Magyars (ethnic Hungarians)
  A: 5
Mansart, Jules Hardouin
  B: 50
Manufacture of war materials
  A: 156–157, 158 (ill.), 165 (ill.),
    166 (ill.)
  See also Industry and
    manufacturing
Maps
  Austria-Hungary, 1914 (ill.)
    A: 18
  Brusilov Offensive (ill.) **A:** 96
  Eastern Front (ill.) **A:** 96, 102
  European political boundaries
    after Treaty of Versailles (ill.)
    A: 203
  European political boundaries
    in 1914 (ill.) **A:** 2
  European possessions prior to
    WWI (ill.) **A:** 10
  first major attacks of WWI (ill.)
    A: 36
  German spring offensive (ill.)
    A: 74
  Germany, 1914 (ill.) **A:** 18
  Hindenburg line (ill.) **A:** 74
  Italian Front (ill.) **A:** 118
  North Sea battles (ill.) **A:** 128

  Ottoman Empire war zones (ill.)
    A: 111
  Schlieffen plan (ill.) **A:** 25
  Serbia (ill.) **A:** 95
  Turkey, 1914 (ill.) **A:** 18
  war zones during WWI (ill.)
    A: 106, 111
  Western Front (ill.) **A:** 37
  Ypres region (ill.) **A:** 64
  Ypres Salient (ill.) **A:** 45
Marianas, the
  A: 106, 107
Marne, Battle of the
  A: 39–40 (ill.)
  B: 52
Marshall, Thomas R.
  B: 172–73
Marshall Islands
  A: 107
Marx, Karl
  B: 63, 70
  PS: 190
Marxism
  PS: 190–191
Masuria, Winter Battle of
  A: 91
Masurian Lakes
  A: 90
Mata Hari
  B: **105–10,** 105 (ill.)
  home of 107 (ill.)
Maximilian (Prince of Baden)
  A: 83
  B: 35
McAdoo, William Gibbs
  A: 179
McCrae, John
  B: 147
Mediterranean Sea, WWI fighting
    in the
  A: 127
Megiddo, Battle of
  A: 118
  B: 7
Mensheviks
  B: 93
Mesopotamia
  A: 117, 122
Messines, Battle of
  PS: 28–30
Meuse-Argonne, Battle of the
  A: 77–80 (ill.)

Mexico, Zimmermann telegram
    sent by Germany to
    A: 174–175
    PS: 93
Michael (grand duke; brother of
    Nicholas II)
    A: 100
    PS: 212
Michel, Victor
    A: 26
Middle East, battles in
    A: 115–117, 117–118
Middle East, strategic
    importance of
    A: 115, 117
Militarism
    B: 68, 73
Military leaders
    Atatürk, Mustafa Kemal B: 6–12
    Foch, Ferdinand B: 48–53, 127
    Haig, Douglas B: 54–61
    Ludendorff, Erich B: 97–104
    Pershing, John Joseph
        B: 51 (ill.), 52, 118–25, 140,
        172–73
    Pétain, Henri-Philippe B: 52,
        126–31
    Richthofen, Manfred von
        (the Red Baron) B: 13–14,
        17, 132–37
Mobilization (preparations for war)
    A: 12, 27–28
    PS: 12–13, 14, 63–64
    in Germany PS: 14, 63
    in Great Britain PS: 11, 12
    in Russia PS: 14, 63
    in the United States PS: 13 (ill.),
        95–96
Modernism (literary movement)
    PS: 114
Mohammed VI
    B: 8
Moltke, Helmuth Johannes von
    A: 33, 39, 88
    B: 99
Monroe Doctrine, the
    B: 172
Mons, Battle of
    A: 37, 38–39
    B: 22, 57
    PS: 43
Montenegro
    A: 10, 13, 92

Morale of British soldiers
    PS: 20–21, 28–30
Morale of German soldiers,
    near end of war
    PS: 41–43
Mörhange-Sarrebourg, Battle of
    A: 137
Morocco
    A: 7, 13, 14
Mortars
    A: 146
Moscow, Russia
    A: 99, 101
    PS: 204–206, 214
Muckraker
    B: 28
Murray, Archibald
    A: 117
Murray, Joseph
    PS: 11
Muslims
    B: 9, 11
Mussolini, Benito
    A: 197, 208
Mustard gas. See Poison gas
Mutinies during WWI
    B: 128–29, 150, 152–55
    PS: 170, 204, 214, 215
    of French army A: 61–62,
        157, 161
    of German navy A: 83, 168–169
    of Russian army A: 99

N

Namibia
    A: 107, 195
Napoléon I (Napoléon Bonaparte)
    B: 49–50, 127
    PS: 2
Napoléon III
    A: 5
National Socialist German
    Workers' Party. See Nazi Party
Nationalistic feelings in Europe
    at beginning of WWI
    A: 14
    PS: 5
Nationalists and nationalism
    B: 66, 73
    German B: 104
    Serbian B: 45
    Slavic B: 46
    Turkish B: 7, 11

Naval strategy during WWI
  A: 123, 127–130, 133–135,
    151–153.
  See also Blockade, naval
Naval strength
  of Austria-Hungary **A:** 6, 11
  of France **A:** 7, 11
  of Germany **A:** 3, 11
  of Great Britain **A:** 7, 9, 11, 113
  of Russia **A:** 11, 12
  of the United States **A:** 14
Naval warfare
  A: 113, 123–135 (ill.)
Nazi Party (Germany)
  A: 28, 193, 197, 204, 206–207
  B: 33, 104, 168, 180
  PS: 135, 144
  conditions leading to rise of the
    B: 154
  occupation of Slavic countries
    by soldiers of the **B:** 46
  persecution of Jewish people
    by the **B:** 75
  policies of the **B:** 69, 74, 83, 130
  political position of the **B:** 64
Neutral countries during WWI
  A: 42, 124, 129, 172
  See also Belgium; United States:
    neutrality of
Neuve-Chapelle
  A: 44
New Deal
  B: 143
"New Freedom" reforms (U.S.)
  B: 169, 172
  PS: 102–103
New Zealand, role of, in WWI
  A: 107, 114–115, 199
Newspaper censorship
  A: 160
Newspapers during WWI
  PS: 169–170
Nicholas (grand duke; cousin
    of Nicholas II)
  A: 94, 95
Nicholas II
  A: 6, 23, 95, 97–99, 100 (ill.)
  B: 166
  PS: 51, 53, 61–62, 62 (ill.), 63,
    68 (ill.), 69, 212
  abdication or overthrow of
    B: 40
  influenced by Alexandra
    B: 34, 93

marriage of **B:** 36
remains of **B:** 95
Nie wieder Krieg ("No more war!")
  B: 73 (ill.)
Nili (Jewish spy ring)
  B: 3–5
*1914–1918: Voices and Images of
    the Great War*
  PS: 9–10, 11, 20–21, 21–22,
    27–30, 43–46
Nivelle, Robert-Georges
  A: 58, 59, 61
  B: 52
Nivelle offensive
  A: 64 (ill.), 65.
  See also Aisne, Second Battle
    of the
No-man's-land
  A: 49, 52 (ill.)
  PS: 18, 19 (ill.)
Nordau, Max
  B: 4
North Africa
  A: 13, 14
North Sea, control of the
  A: 127–130
Novels about WWI
  PS: 128
  *See also All Quiet on the Western
    Front; A Farewell to Arms*
Nurses in WWI
  B: 23–25
Nurses on the Western Front,
    perspective of
  PS: 39–42
Nurses, recruitment of, for
    war effort
  PS: 171, 183 (ill.), 186 (ill.)

O

Offensives. *See* Battles
Office of War Information
  B: 28, 33
Oil wells in the Persian Gulf,
    strategic importance of
  A: 115
Omdurman, battles of
  B: 56
Opinion, public. *See* Civilian
    attitudes toward WWI
Orlando, Vittorio
  A: 190
  B: 175

Otavi
  A: 108
Ottoman Empire
  B: 3, 6–7, 9, 86, 87
  PS: 103, 107
  area ruled by A: 13, 109
  end of A: 118, 195
  goals of, in WWI A: 203
  strategic importance of A: 109
  war zones in A: 111 (ill.)
  See also Turkey
Ourcq, River
  A: 40
Owen, Wilfred
  B: **111–17**, 111 (ill.), 147
  PS: 2, 113, 122 (ill.), 129
  attitude of, toward WWI
    PS: 118, 121–122
  background and war experience
    of PS: 123, 130
  poems by PS: **122–124,
    124–125, 126–128**
  popularity of poems by PS: 122

P

Pacific, battles on islands in the
  A: 106–107, 122
Pacifists
  PS: 143
Pacifists who fought in WWI
  B: 111, 113
Paléologue, Maurice
  A: 28
Palestine
  A: 118, 122
  British role in B: 3, 5, 87
  history of Jewish settlement in
    B: 1–2, 4
  Jewish homeland in B: 3–4, 87
Palmer, A. Mitchell
  B: 82, 176
Palmer Raids
  B: 82
Pankhurst, A. D.
  PS: 43–45
Parachutes
  A: 149
Paris Peace Conference
  A: 189–192, 196
  B: 16, 87–88, 170, 174
Paśa. *See* Cemal Paśa, Ahmed

Passchendaele, Battle of
  A: 63–65
  B: 17, 23, 58
Passionate Prodigality, A
  PS: 13
Patriotism in Europe at beginning
    of WWI
  PS: 5
Peace
  A: 196–197.
  See also Armistice agreements;
    Armistice celebrations
Peace (poem)
  PS: 119
Peace celebrations
  PS: 38 (ill.), 44 (ill.)
  See also World War I: end of
Peace plan. *See* Fourteen
    Points, the
Peace treaty ending WWI
  B: 166, 169, 176
  PS: 39, 59, 82
Pégoud, Adolphe
  A: 148, 149
People's Republican
    Party (Turkey)
  B: 11
Pershing, John Joseph
  A: 67–68 (ill.), 73, 76, 181
  B: 51 (ill.), 52, **118–25**, 118
    (ill.), 121 (ill.), 140, 172–73
  PS: 98
Persian Gulf, strategic
    importance of
  A: 115
Persian Gulf War (1991)
  B: 180
Pétain, Henri-Philippe
  A: 45, 51, 61, 68 (ill.)
  B: 52, **126–31**, 126 (ill.),
    128 (ill.)
Petrograd, Russia
  A: 99, 101
  PS: 207–211, 214
Phosgene gas
  A: 76, 143 (ill.), 144
  See also Poison gas
Pilots. *See* Aces (fighter pilots)
Planes. *See* Airplanes
Plekhanov, Georgy
  B: 92
Plumer, Herbert
  A: 62

Poems about WWI
   B: 111–13, 147
   PS: 115–130 (*see also* Brooke,
      Rupert; Owen, Wilfred;
      Sassoon, Siegfried; Seeger,
      Alan; War poetry)
   Anthem for Doomed Youth
      124–125
   Counter-Attack 125–126
   The Dead **PS:** 119–120
   Dulce Et Decorum Est 126–128
   I Have a Rendezvous with Death
      PS: 120
   Peace **PS:** 118–119
   Sonnet X 120–121
   *Sonnet XI: On Returning to the
      Front After Leave* 121
   Strange Meeting **PS:** 122–124
   They **PS:** 124
Poetry, importance of, during WWI
   PS: 115–118
Pogroms
   A: 205
   B: 2
Poison gas
   A: 46, 70, 144
   B: 114, 116 (ill.)
   PS: 2, 127 (ill.)
   Allied use of **A:** 47, 76, 78,
      143–144
   casualties caused by **A:** 144
   effects of **A:** 46, 58 (ill.),
      142–143, 144
   first use of **A:** 45, 46, 141–142
   German use of **A:** 50, 70,
      141–142
Poland
   PS: 103, 107, 166, 189, 191
   battles between Germany and
      Russia in **A:** 90, 93–94
   independence granted to
      A: 101, 188, 204
   postwar events in **A:** 194,
      197, 204
   strategic position of **A:** 86
Political cartoons
   PS: 54 (ill.), 84 (ill.)
Political leaders
   Atatürk, Mustafa Kemal **B:** 6–12
   Franz Ferdinand **B:** 42–47
   Jaurès, Jean **B:** 62–67
   Lenin, Vladimir **B:** 82,
      90–96, 102

Pétain, Henri-Philippe **B:** 52,
   126–31
Wilson, Woodrow **B:** 23, 27, 29,
   31, 122, 169–77
Population of European countries
   in 1913. *See* individual
   countries
Population of the United States
   in 1913
   A: 14
Posters promoting the war effort.
   See Propaganda posters;
   Recruiting posters
Potiorek, Oscar
   A: 91
   B: 45–46
Pound, Ezra
   PS: 128, 146
Prager, Robert
   A: 177
Princip, Gavrilo
   A: 1, 17–18, 19 (ill.), 20–21 (ill.)
   B: 42, 46
Pripet Marshes
   A: 90, 96, 97
Prisoners of war, experiences of,
   at end of WWI
   PS: 45–46
Prittwitz, Max von
   A: 88
Progressive reforms in the
   United States
   PS: 102–103
Proletariats
   B: 155
Propaganda
   A: 159–161 (ill.), 173 (ill.),
      176–178, 179, 207
   B: 19, 25, 29–30, 135, 163 (ill.),
      166 (ill.)
   PS: 7, 12, 99, 166, 169–171
Propaganda posters
   A: 161 (ill.), 173 (ill.), 179
   PS: 166, **169–188**
   in France **PS:** 174 (ill.), 176
      (ill.), 179 (ill.), 186 (ill.)
   in Germany **PS:** 180 (ill.)
   in Great Britain **PS:** 182 (ill.),
      184 (ill.)
   in Russia **PS:** 173 (ill.), 185 (ill.)
   in the United States **PS:** 170
      (ill.), 175 (ill.), 178 (ill.),
      181 (ill.)

Prussia
A: 2
B: 98, 100, 164, 167
PS: 53
See also East Prussia
Psychological stress caused
by WWI
PS: 34
Public opinion. *See* Civilian
attitudes toward WWI
Putnik, Radomir
A: 92

Q

Quénault, Louis
A: 148, 151

R

Radicals and radicalism
B: 64, 69, 82, 152
Railway systems, importance of,
during WWI
A: 12, 25, 28, 78, 92, 158–159
PS: 14
Rasputin, Grigory
A: 93, 94 (ill.), 96, 98–99
B: 38–39, 39 (ill.), 93
Rathenau, Walther
A: 156
PS: 201
Rationing of food during WWI
A: 162–164, 178
PS: 165, 179 (ill.), 202 (ill.)
See also Food shortages
during WWI
Reactionaries
B: 64
Reconnaissance (information-
gathering) missions
PS: 22–27
Recruiting posters
PS: 6 (ill.), 7, 12
in Austria PS: 177 (ill.)
in France PS: 174 (ill.)
in Great Britain PS: 172 (ill.)
in the United States
PS: 183 (ill.)
Red Army
B: 41, 82, 93
PS: 214

Red Baron, the. *See* Richthofen,
Manfred von
Red Cross. *See* American Red Cross
Red Scare, the
B: 82
Reds, the. *See* Red Army
Reed, John
B: 145
Refugees
Jewish B: 1–2
produced by WWI A: 157 (ill.),
163 (ill.), 200; PS: 47
Reichstag Investigating
Committee
B: 150–51
Reinsurance Treaty of 1887
A: 3
Remarque, Erich Maria
PS: 113, 114, **131–134**,
132 (ill.), 145
background of PS: 134–135
novels by PS: 144
postwar attitudes reflected in
war novels by PS: 128, 131
success of PS: 131
WWI service of PS: 134, 144
Rennenkampf, Pavel
A: 87, 88, 90
Reparations
A: 192, 202
Resistance movement in Belgium
B: 22, 24–25
Revolution. *See* Russia: revolution
in; Workers' (people's)
revolution
Richthofen, Manfred von
(the Red Baron)
A: 149
B: 13–14, 17, **132–37**, 132 (ill.)
Rickenbacker, Eddie
A: 149
B: **138–43**, 138 (ill.), 140 (ill.),
142 (ill.)
Right, the
B: 64–65
Romania
A: 97, 199
PS: 63
Romanian Front
A: 110 (ill.)
Romanov family
B: 36

Roosevelt, Franklin D.
  B: 143, 177
Roosevelt, Theodore
  B: 120, 148, 171–72, 175
  PS: 102
Rosenberg, Isaac
  B: 112–13
  PS: 117
Rosenthal, Moriz
  B: 78
Ross, Alexander
  B: 16
Ross, Robert
  B: 115
Rouvroy, Claude Henri de
  B: 63
Rudolf (Austrian archduke)
  B: 43
Russia
  alliances of **A:** 3, 5–6, 7, 24;
    PS: 50, 54, 58, 59
  armistice signed by **PS:** 214
  army problems and revolt in
    A: 86, 99
  assassination of royal family in
    PS: 69
  casualty rate and soldiers killed
    in combat **A:** 199, 200
  civil war in **B:** 41, 93–94;
    PS: 214
  Communist government in
    A: 197, 206; **PS:** 214
  conscription (military draft) in
    PS: 8
  economy of **A:** 8–9, 93, 97, 197,
    206; **PS:** 167, 202
  food shortage in **PS:** 167,
    202–203, 205, 207
  goals of, in WWI **A:** 203
  government of, prior to WWI
    A: 6
  industry and manufacturing in
    A: 12, 97
  massacre of striking workers in
    PS: 191, 203
  military and naval strength of
    A: 9, 11, 12
  offensives **A:** 86–91, 100–101
  patriotism in, at beginning of
    WWI **PS:** 5
  population of **A:** 12, 97
  propaganda posters in
    PS: 173 (ill.), 185 (ill.)

provisional government in
    PS: 212
  revolution in **A:** 97, 99–101,
    197, 204–206 (ill.); **B:** 38,
    39–41, 93, 102, 166; **PS:** 59,
    69, 167, 198, 203–214
  royal family of **A:** 100 (ill.);
    B: 40–41
  strikes, protests, and labor
    disputes in **PS:** 167, 191, 203
  WWI peace treaty signed by
    B: 93
  WWI unpopular in **B:** 39
  See also Russian army;
    Soviet Union
Russian army
  casualty rate of **PS:** 39
  mobilization of **PS:** 14
  mutiny of **PS:** 204
  size of **PS:** 8
Russian Social Democratic
    Workers' Party
  B: 92
Russner, Kathe
  PS: 39–42
Russo-Japanese War (1904–05)
  B: 38, 120, 175

S

Sagittarius Rising
  PS: 22–27, 37
Saint-Mihiel
  A: 75, 77, 181
  PS: 98
St. Petersburg
  A: 28
Salandra, Antonio
  A: 119
Salonika Front
  A: 102
Sambre River
  A: 37
Samoa
  A: 107
Samsonov, Aleksandr
  A: 87–89
Sarajevo
  A: 16, 21, 91
Sassoon, Siegfried
  B: 112–13, 115–16, 147
  PS: 2, 113, 123, 129 (ill.)
  attitude of, toward WWI
    PS: 118, 121–122, 128

background and war experience
of **PS:** 129
poems by **PS:** 124, **125–126**
popularity of poems by **PS:** 122
Scheer, Reinhard
   A: 131, 132
Schetter, Hans Otto
   PS: 27–28
Schiller, Friedrich
   B: 70
Schlieffen, Alfred von
   A: 24, 32
   B: 98
   PS: 71
Schlieffen plan
   A: 24–26 (ill.), 32–33, 38, 39
   PS: 71–73
Scott-Moncrieff, Charles
   B: 115
SDKP (Social Democracy for the
   Kingdom of Poland)
   PS: 190, 191
Seeger, Alan
   B: 144–49, 144 (ill.)
   PS: 113, 123
   attitude of, toward WWI
    PS: 117, 118
   background and war experience
   of **PS:** 88, 119, 128, 130
   poems by **PS: 120–121**
   popularity of poems by **PS:** 122
Selective Service Administration
   (U.S.)
   A: 180
   B: 173
   PS: 14
Separate peace, treaties
   preventing a
   PS: 59
Serbia
   A: 95 (ill.)
   B: 42, 45
   PS: 54, 64, 107
   allies of **A:** 9–10
   Austro-Hungarian ultimatum to
    PS: 63
   battles in **A:** 91–93
   casualties **A:** 92, 199
   conflict with Austria-Hungary
    A: 13, 16, 19–23, 91–92
   postwar events in **A:** 194
   postwar (Fourteen Points) plan
   for **PS:** 107

role of, in WWI **PS:** 50, 58,
   61, 68
WWI battles in **PS:** 69
Serre, battle at
   PS: 123
Sèvres, Treaty of
   A: 195
   B: 8–9
Shell shock
   PS: 34, 123, 129
Shipping, WWI effects on
   merchant
   A: 133–135, 151, 162, 173
   See also Blockade, naval
Ships. *See* Weapons: battleships;
   Weapons: dreadnoughts
Siegfried Zone
   A: 59
Sitting Bull
   B: 119
Slack, C. M.
   PS: 45–46
Slavic countries, unification of
   B: 45–46
Social Democracy for the
   Kingdom of Poland (SDKP)
   PS: 190, 191
Social Democratic Party of
   Germany (SPD)
   PS: 191, 192
Social Democrats
   A: 83
Socialism and socialist movement
   B: 28, 63–65, 69–70, 82,
   102, 152
   PS: 167, 189, 191, 197
Socialist groups
   A: 12, 83, 157, 176, 206
Socialist view of WWI
   PS: 191, 194–197, 215
Soldiers
   American (ill.) **A:** 33, 34, 191
   Bishop, William Avery **B:** 13–18
   British (ill.) **A:** 191
   French (ill.) **A:** 35, 40, 52, 152
   German (ill.) **A:** 17, 38, 43,
   89, 195
   Italian (ill.) **A:** 119
   killed in WWI **A:** 199. *See also*
   Casualties
   Lawrence, T. E. (Lawrence of
   Arabia) **B:** 84–89
   leaving home (Germany) (ill.)
   A: 17

Owen, Wilfred **B:** 111–17, 147
Rickenbacker, Eddie **B:** 138–43
Seeger, Alan **B:** 144–49
Stumpf, Richard **B:** 150–56
York, Alvin C. **B:** 178–83
See also Military leaders
Solomon Islands
    A: 107
*Some Desperate Glory: The World
    War I Diary of a British
    Officer, 1917*
    PS: 12
Somme, Battle of the
    A: 49, 52–54, 79
    B: 52, 58–59, 111, 113
    PS: 20–21, 21–27, 119
Sonnet X
    PS: 120–121
*Sonnet XI: On Returning to the Front
    After Leave*
    PS: 121
Sophie (countess; wife of Franz
    Ferdinand)
    A: 16–17
    B: 42–44 , 44 (ill.)
    PS: 50 (ill.)
South Africa, Union of
    A: 108
Soviet Union
    A: 206
    B: 74, 90, 95
    PS: 214
    See also Russia
Soviets
    PS: 213
Spanish Flu
    A: 169
Spanish-American War (1898)
    B: 120
Spartacus League
    PS: 191, 197, 215
SPD (Social Democratic Party) of
    Germany
    PS: 191, 192
Spee, Maximilian von
    A: 125
Spring offensive
    A: 67, 68–73, 74 (ill.)
Spy activity (intelligence) during
    WWI
    B: 1, 3–5, 85, 105, 108–10, 122
Stalin, Joseph
    A: 206

Stallupönen
    A: 87
Starvation. *See* Food shortage
    during WWI
Statute of Westminster (1931)
    B: 16
Stein, Gertrude
    PS: 146
Stewart, Carson
    PS: 9–10
*Storm of Steel: From the Diary of a
    German Storm-Troop Officer on
    the Western Front*
    PS: 31–34, 42–43
Strange Meeting
    PS: 122–124
Strategy. *See* Eastern Front:
    strategy on the; Naval
    strategy during WWI; War
    plans; Western Front: strategy
    used on the
Strikes. *See* Labor protests
Stumpf, Richard
    B: 150–56
Submarine attacks
    B: 101, 166, 172–73
    on the *Lusitania* **PS:** 7, 92 (ill.)
    on U.S. ships **PS:** 79, 80, 87,
        92, 103
    purpose of **PS:** 93, 103
    U.S. condemnation of
        PS: 94–95
    See also Weapons: submarines
Suez Canal, strategic
    importance of
    A: 117
Suffrage, women's
    PS: 187
Sukhomlinov, V. A.
    A: 87
Surrender of Germany
    PS: 98, 109 (ill.)
    See also Armistice agreements
Susse x pledge
    A: 174
Swinton, Ernest D.
    A: 146
Sykes-Picot Agreement
    B: 87, 89
Syria
    B: 3

T

Taft, William Howard
  B: 171
  PS: 102
Tanks. *See* Weapons: tanks
Tannenberg, Battle of
  A: 88–90 (ill.), 94
  B: 100–01
Tanzania
  A: 107, 195
Taxes. *See* United States: income
  tax reform in
Tear gas
  A: 46
  See also Poison gas
Technology. *See* Factories; Gas
  masks; Weapons
Telegram from Germany to
  Mexico. *See* Zimmermann
  Telegram.
Telegrams from American
  consulates in Russia
  PS: 167, **204–211**
Telegrams of Nicholas II and
  Wilhelm II. *See* Willy-Nicky
  Telegrams
They
  PS: **124**
Thomas, Edward
  B: 113, 157–59, 161
Thomas, Helen
  B: 113, **157–62**
Tirpitz, Alfred von
  B: 166
Tito, Josip Broz
  A: 21
  B: 46
Togo
  A: 107
Tolstoy, Leo
  B: 70
Total war
  PS: 164
Townshend, C. V. F.
  A: 116–117
Trade, alliances and importance of
  A: 172–173, 183
Trains. *See* Railway systems,
  importance of
Treaties
  Brest-Litovsk, Treaty of **PS:** 214
  ending WWI **A:** 187, 193,
    194, 196

  Lausanne **B:** 9
  Reinsurance Treaty of 1887 **A:** 3
  secrecy of **PS:** 55, 59, 105
  Sèvres **A:** 195; **B:** 8–9
  Versailles **A:** 171, 184, 192–194,
    196, 206, 207, 208; **B:** 52,
    169, 174
  See also Alliances; Armistice
    agreements
Trench warfare during WWI
  A: 50 (ill.), 77, 144
  B: 58–59
  PS: 17–18, 28–30, 77
  French and British soldiers in
    trenches **PS:** 18 (ill.)
  German innovations in **A:** 47,
    53
  German soldiers in trenches
    PS: 19 (ill.), 77 (ill.), 137 (ill.)
  illustrations of trenches (ill.)
    A: 34, 35, 72, 138, 141, 152
  Italian soldiers in trenches
    PS: 155 (ill.)
  strategy and weapons used in
    A: 41, 140, 146
Trenchard, Hugh M.
  B: 15
Trialism
  B: 44–45
Triple Alliance
  PS: 50, 59
Triple Entente
  A: 1, 7, 10, 11, 14
Trotsky, Leon
  A: 101
  B: 93, 102
  PS: 214
Truce. *See* Armistice agreements;
  Christmas Truce
Tsingtao
  A: 107, 124
Turenne, Henri de La Tour
  B: 50
Turkey
  PS: 32–33, 37, 63
  alliance with Germany **A:** 127
  Armenian genocide in **A:** 111,
    112, 198; **B:** 3; **PS:** 32–33, 37
  armistice agreement signed by
    A: 82, 118, 194
  battles in **A:** 105, 109–113
  borders of, 1914 **A:** 18 (ill.)
  casualties **A:** 111, 115, 199

clothing regulations in
   B: 7, 9, 10
ethnic minorities in **B:** 3, 11
government and religious
   customs in **B:** 9–10
Grand National Assembly
   established in **B:** 8–9
independence gained by
   B: 6, 8–9
Kurdish rebellion in **B:** 11
legal system in **B:** 9–10
modernization of **B:** 9–11
nationalism in **B:** 11
postwar events in **A:** 208
strategic importance of
   A: 109, 113, 115
surrender of **A:** 103
women's status in **B:** 10
Turks marching during
   World War I
   B: 8 (ill.)
Twelfth Battle of the Isonzo
   A: 120

U

U-boats. *See* Submarine attacks
Union of Soviet Socialist
   Republics (U.S.S.R.).
   See Soviet Union.
Unions, workers'. *See* Labor
   protests
United Kingdom. *See* Great Britain
United Nations
   A: 196
   B: 175
   PS: 110
United States
   African Americans, treatment
      and role of, during WWI
      A: 177, 180 (ill.), 182–183
   alliances before entry into
      WWI **A:** 9
   anti-German hysteria in **B:** 32
   as world power **B:** 175;
      PS: 47, 79
   attitudes about WWI **A:**
      171–172, 174, 176–178,
      179–180, 183–184
   battles involving U.S. troops
      A: 71, 73–75, 75–77, 79–80
      (ill.), 81 (ill.), 181

casualty rate of. *See* Allies:
   casualty rate of
conscription (military draft) in
   PS: 14, 99
Declaration of Neutrality
   PS: 81, **86–87**
declaration of war by
   PS: 97, 98 (ill.)
economy of, during WWI **A:** 9,
   174, 185, 208; **PS:** 87–88,
   165–166
English-only laws passed in
   B: 32
entry into WWI **A:** 67, 135,
   152, 171, 174–175
European ties of **PS:** 84–85, 86
foreign policy of **PS:** 79–81,
   82, 93
foreign trade by, early in WWI
   PS: 80, 87, 88, 91, 101
German aggression directed at
   PS: 91, 92, 103
German Americans, treatment
   of, during WWI **A:** 177
income tax reform in **PS:** 103
industry and manufacturing in
   A: 14, 178–179
isolationism in **A:** 183–185,
   196, 208; **B:** 170; **PS:** 80, 82,
   83, 103, 109
leftist politics in **B:** 82
military draft in **B:** 173
military and naval strength of
   A: 14
neutrality of, at beginning of
   WWI **A:** 172–174; **B:** 172;
   PS: 79, 81, 86–87, 91, 95,
   96, 103
peace celebrations in
   PS: 38 (ill.)
policies and propaganda during
   wartime **A:** 175–178
population of **A:** 14
postwar difficulties in **B:** 176
progressive reforms in
   PS: 102–103
prohibition in **B:** 177
propaganda agency created by
   PS: 99
propaganda posters in
   PS: 170 (ill.), 175 (ill.),
   178 (ill.), 181 (ill.)

recruiting posters in
   PS: 7, 183 (ill.)
role of, since World War II
   B: 175
soldiers (ill.) **A:** 33, 34, 191;
   PS: 13 (ill.)
trade policy during WWI
   A: 172–173
war information agency **A:** 177
War Message **PS:** 81, **94–97**
women's voting rights in
   B: 177; **PS:** 187
WWI battles involving soldiers
   from **PS:** 98
United States Information Agency
   B: 28

V

Vauban, Sébastien
   B: 50
Vaughan, Edwin Campion
   PS: 12
Vaux, Fort
   A: 50, 51
Verdun, Battle of
   A: 49–51
   B: 97, 128, 130, 133
Versailles, Treaty of
   A: 171, 184, 192–194, 196,
     206, 207, 208
   B: 52, 176
   PS: 39, 59, 82, 108, 109, 110
Versailles Peace Conference
   PS: 105 (ill.)
Victoria (queen of Great Britain)
   B: 35–36, 38, 163
Villa, Francisco "Pancho"
   B: 121–22, 172
Villain, Raoul
   B: 67
Vimy Ridge
   A: 45–46, 47, 62
   B: 15–16
Voting rights for women
   A: 164, 165
   PS: 187

W

Wadi Run
   B: 87

War bonds
   B: 30 (ill.), 32
   PS: 166, 169, 173 (ill.),
     174 (ill.), 175 (ill.), 176 (ill.),
     181 (ill.)
   posters promoting purchase of
     A: 161 (ill.), 173 (ill.), 179
War Council for the Red Cross
   B: 23
War effort. *See* Civilian war effort
War Message (Wilson)
   PS: 81, **94–97**
War novels
   PS: 128 (see also *All Quiet on
     the Western Front; A Farewell
     to Arms*)
War plans
   A: 24–27, 43–46, 67–69, 92
   B: 52, 58, 123, 127–28, 133
   PS: 51, 71–73
War poets and poetry
   B: 111–13, 147
   PS: 113, **115–118**
   See also Brooke, Rupert;
     Owen, Wilfred; Poems about
     WWI; Sassoon, Siegfried;
     Seeger, Alan
War resistance movement in
   Belgium
   B: 22, 24–25
War zones during WWI
   A: 106 (ill.), 111 (ill.)
Warfare, types of. *See* Airplanes;
   Cavalry; Naval warfare;
   Trench warfare; Weapons
Wars
   Balkan Wars **A:** 194
   Boer War **A:** 39
   Franco-Prussian War
     A: 3, 5, 159
   Great War, the **A:** 1
Warships. *See* Weapons:
   battleships; Weapons:
   dreadnoughts
Weapons
   A: 114 (ill.), 116 (ill.)
   artillery **A:** 29, 44, 50, 53,
     70–71, 146, 167
   barbed wire **A:** 33 (ill.), 41, 49,
     53–54, 140; **PS:** 18
   battleships **A:** 11 (ill.), 113,
     124 (ill.), 131 (ill.), 151

bombs, mines, and explosives
A: 62, 113, 130, 135, 146,
147, 148
dreadnoughts (battleships)
A: 124 (ill.), 125, 131,
132, 151
flamethrower A: 49, 50,
121 (ill.), 144
howitzer (ill.) A: 32
machine guns A: 41, 48,
138–141 (ill.)
mortars A: 146
submarines (U-boats) A: 76,
124, 133–135 (ill.), 151–153,
162, 173–175, 194
tanks A: 54, 65, 66 (ill.), 140,
145–147 (ill.); PS: 2
zeppelins A: 147, 167, 168 (ill.)
See also Airplanes; Poison gas
Weapons, introduction of new
PS: 2
Weapons, production of, vs. food
production
PS: 187
Weather, battlefield conditions
and
A: 63, 92–93, 108, 111,
113, 116
Weimar Republic
PS: 198
Welt-politik (world scheme)
A: 7
Western Front
PS: 17, 77
first years on the A: 31–55
location/extent of the
A: 37 (ill.), 38, 57
strategy used on the
A: 44, 57–59, 65–69,
138–139, 140, 181
Westminster, Statute of (1931)
B: 16
White Army (the Whites)
B: 41, 93
PS: 214
Wilhelm I
A: 3
B: 41, 93, 163–64, 167
PS: 53
Wilhelm II
A: 3, 5, 7, 8 (ill.), 13, 22, 29, 83,
87 (ill.), 123

B: 19, 71, 97, 99, 100–01,
163–68, 163 (ill.)
PS: 51, 61–62, 62 (ill.), 63,
69, 84 (ill.)
Willy-Nicky Telegrams
PS: 51, 61, 62, **64–68**
Wilson, Woodrow
A: 184 (ill.), 185, 189 (ill.)
B: 23, 27, 29, **169–77**, 169 (ill.),
174 (ill.)
PS: 81 (ill.), 84 (ill.), 87, 105
(ill.), 110 (ill.), 212
Declaration of Neutrality by
PS: 81, 85, **86–87**, 91
declaration of war by A:
174–176; PS: 81, 92–93
downfall of PS: 108–110
and Fourteen Points A:
182–183, 187, 188; PS: 82,
101–104, **104–108**
League of Nations proposed by
A: 183–184; PS: 82, 103, 104
military draft instituted by
PS: 99
neutrality urged by A: 172
opinion about colonies A: 195
peace conference role of
A: 189–191, 196
progressive reforms supported
by PS: 102–103
War Message PS: 81, **94–97**
Windhoek
A: 108
Winter Battle of Masuria
A: 91
Women
effects of WWI on
PS: 32–33, 47
role of, during WWI
A: 164–166 (ill.); PS: 164
(ill.), 164–165, 171,
183–186 (ill.), 188
voting rights of A: 164, 165;
B: 177; PS: 187
Women's Land Army
PS: 164
Women's roles during WWI
Aaronsohn, Sarah B: 1–5
Cavell, Edith B: 19–26
Fyodorovna, Alexandra B:
34–41
Kollwitz, Käthe B: 68–76
Mata Hari B: 105–10
Thomas, Helen B: 113, 157–62

Women's status in Turkey
  B: 10
Workers' (people's) revolution
  PS: 166, 189, 191, 192, 197, 198
Workmen's compensation
    law (U.S.)
  PS: 102
Works Progress Administration
    (WPA)
  B: 33
World War I
  attitudes toward, early in war
    PS: 2, 5–7, 9–10, 12, 172 (ill.),
    174 (ill.), 192–197
  attitudes toward, later in war
    PS: 13, 150–152 (fiction),
    154–156 (fiction), 166,
    175 (ill.)
  battlefield conditions during
    B: 116 (ill.)
  beginnings of **A:** 23–24;
    B: 42, 165–66; **PS:** 68,
    72 (ill.), 76, 77
  casualties caused by **A:** 199,
    200 (ill.); **PS:** 34, 38–39
  causes of (general) **PS:** 1
  censorship during **PS:** 12, 169
  civilian war effort during
    A: 155–169
  costs of, financial **A:** 198,
    201–202
  deaths caused by **PS:** 37, 47
  effects of, on civilians **A:** 82
    (ill.), 129, 147, 157 (ill.),
    161–164 (ill.), 198, 200;
    PS: 47, 163–166
  end of **PS:** 37–46, 111
  financial cost of **PS:** 165
  goals of European countries in
    A: 202–203
  influence of, on literature and
    worldview **PS:** 114, 131,
    145, 148
  peace treaty ending **PS:** 39,
    59, 82
  popular opinion against
    A: 12–13, 14, 99, 101.
    (*see also* Civilian attitudes
    toward WWI)
  U.S. declaration of war during
    PS: 97, 98 (ill.)
  war plans for **A:** 24–27, 43–46,
    67–69, 92

war zones during **A:** 106 (ill.),
    111 (ill.)
  See also Food shortage during
    WWI; Mobilization
World War II
  A: 185, 197, 199, 202, 204, 208
Wounded soldiers, numbers of
  PS: 34
  See also Casualties caused by
    WWI
WPA. *See* Works Progress
    Administration.

Y

Yekaterinburg
  B: 40–41
YMCA assistance during WWI
  B: 23
York, Alvin C.
  B: 178–83, 178 (ill.)
  film about, scene from
    182 (ill.)
Young Bosnians
  B: 46
Young Turks
  A: 112
Ypres, First Battle of
  A: 41
  B: 52, 57
Ypres Salient and region (ill.)
  A: 45, 64
Ypres, Second Battle of
  A: 45, 46
Ypres, Third Battle of
  A: 63–65
  PS: 27–28
Yudenich, Nikolay
  A: 113
Yugoslavia
  A: 194, 197, 204
  B: 46

Z

Zangwill, Israel
  B: 4
Zelle, Margaretha Geertruida.
    See Mata Hari
Zeppelin, destruction caused by
  A: 82 (ill.).